MAKING MOCKUPS

Create stunning and unique mockups for products, editorial illustration and marketing using free AI and Adobe Photoshop

by Susan Bonser

Making Mockups
Create stunning and unique mockups using free Dall-e and Adobe Photoshop

ISBN: 9798334368002
Imprint: Independently published

You can email us at info@art-type.com.
See our work at https://art-type.com
Instructional videos of this at youtube.com/@ART-TYPE

Contents

Mockup for a beach towel and deck shoes

First, I used the product images as the manufacturer created them rather than use my design art for the pattern. In this way the art is properly scaled to the product—hopefully avoiding buyer disappointment or surprise. They expect to get what is in the picture when they make the purchase.

I had a concept, an idea in mind for the photo. I wanted a modern lounge chair at the side of a swimming pool, minimalist modern environment. These were the terms then that I used to generate the AI images that became the basis for the finished photo. I specified in the prompt that I wanted the towel lying on the lounge chair to be plain white.

I generate a lot of images to get to the best one to use. It is not unusual for me to pull fifty images or more for a single mockup. In addition to looking for the image to be the content I specified, I look for a good quality image. AI is often generated from compressed images, then compressed again when they are delivered to you so frequently full of JPG artifacts. There are some things you can do to get rid of a little compression ugliness, but the better choice is to start with the best quality image possible.

Above, finished image in the proportions it was designed. Right, close-up of the finished image showing the beach towel and deck shoes products in position.

STEPS

1. The original AI generation.

2. The manufacturer's product shot of the beach towel with the background removed, in this case the white background. It was not necessary with this rectangle, but I often make a mask for the shape of the product before I delete the background. Using a mask has a couple of advantages. First I can fiddle the edges. Also, if I am doing multiple of the same object I can reuse the mask and don't have to make a new one every time. The shoes are an example of where I would make a mask.

3. In Photoshop I use the Edit>Transform tools to scale, shape, and fit the towel roughly to the white towel in the original AI.

4. Then here's the trick. I create a mask for the white towel on the AI chair. Then I copy and paste that towel on a new layer. I make sure the product image is covering the AI white towel, then select the outside of the white towel and delete from the outside of the product towel so the images on the two layers fit over each other exactly.

5. With the product towel on a layer under the AI white towel, I select Multiply in the Layer menu and reduce the opacity until I like the way it looks. This puts the shadows and shape of the white towel onto the product towel.

6. I position the deck shoes where I want them in the photo. Then, 7 through 9, I put a shadow under the shoes, and then on top of the shoes to match the environmental shadow on the floor.

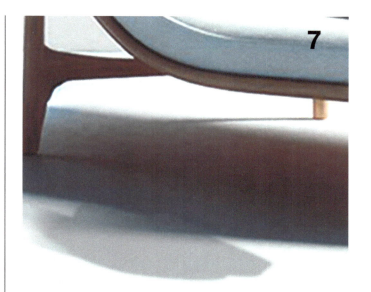

Additional similar examples

Here are a couple of examples similar to the swimming pool picture. In both, the small pictures are the original AI generations. The same technique was used to replace the white towel with the product pattern and to place a scarf in a frame over the bathtub. I did not use the towel in the original AI generation, but copied it from another AI generated image in the teal bathroom image.

In the chair picture, I used the white afghan and pillow to place the ladybug product patterns. The key is to generate images that have white areas where you want to replace the pattern, texture, color with your product pattern. A mask was

created of the pillow area then used to trim the product pattern image, and finally placed on a layer over the pattern with a layer setting of "Multiply" to put the shape and shadows of the original on the new pattern. I often change the opacity of the copy of the original section. Sometimes I increase the contrast to make the shadows really pop. I often reduce the saturation so color from the AI doesn't contaminate my pattern.

You will also notice that in both of these pictures, I extended the backgrounds. The original AI generation was a square and I needed a horizontal format for the layout design. I will demonstrate that specifically in a later section.

Mockup for a shoe with a scrunched sock

Here is an example that is a little more involved. You always have to weigh the time it will take to accomplish something versus the time people will spend looking at it to make a buying decision. Still, the time and expense it takes to produce an image this way is far less costly than the traditional method of hiring a model, booking a studio and a photographer—not to mention a stylist, hair dresser/makeup, coffee, lunch, messengers, etc. This way of producing images is faster and a whole lot cheaper. Even if you spend a good amount of time on it.

The manufacturer's image of the product was a mid-calf length sock shot flat overhead and worn by a male model on a hairy leg. I envisioned a more stylish presentation, with the sock scrunched down around the ankle in a fun shoe. I demonstrate producing this image in a Croc-type shoe and include examples of some other shoe styles using the same technique.

This image required a couple of different AI generations. First, I generated an image of a close-up of a leg in a shoe. Then, I also needed an image of a white sock scrunched up on an ankle.

The original AI generation is shown above. The finished image is shown at the right.

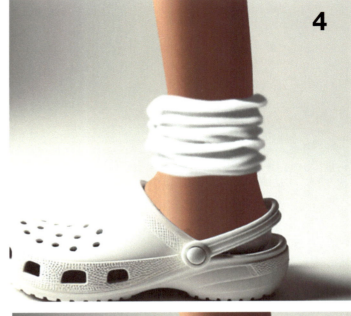

STEPS

1. The original AI generation.

2. The manufacturer's product shot with the background removed. Again, this product shot was flat against a white background so it was easy to select and remove it.

3. I generated a white sock scrunched down on an ankle with no shoe.

4. I isolated the section of the sock I wanted to use and pasted in onto a layer. I sized and positioned the scrunch on the ankle then locked the layer.

5. I selected and copied a section of the foot of the sock. I sized and shaped it to realistically fit the ankle in the shoe picture.

6. First I selected a piece of the product sock image and positioned it over the scrunch layer, making sure it was sized so that it covered the scrunch. The next step was to select a section of the scrunch, then copy that shape from the product image and paste it onto a new layer "In Place".

7. Working back and forth between the scrunch layer and the product image layer, I selected one section of the scrunch at a time and pasted it "In Place" into a new layer until all of the ripples of the scrunched sock were completed.

8. I created a band for the top of the sock and some shadowing for the back of the ankle.

9. The last step was to make sure the original scrunch AI layer was over the new product scrunches, then select "Multiply" in the layers menu and adjust the opacity of the white AI scrunch layer until it looks right. This step puts all of the shape and shadows from the original AI scrunch onto the new product scrunch image layers.

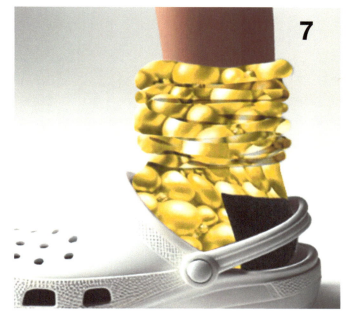

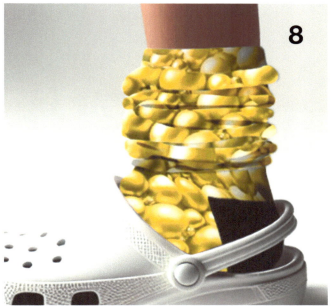

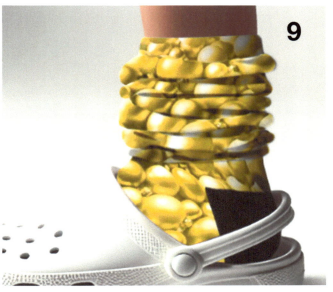

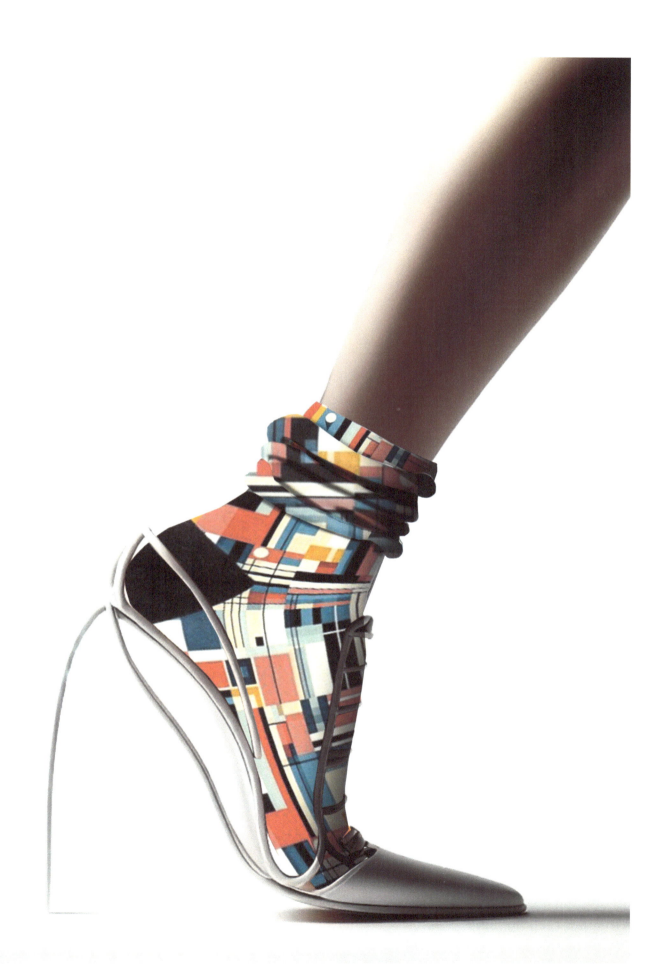

Mockup for an allover patterned t-shirt

My impression of most mockup software is that the image of the product is sometimes placed awkwardly in backgrounds and the overall effect just looks wrong. Models shot in studio placed on Hawaiian sunset beaches. The lighting is inconsistent; it just looks discordant. The way we are doing it here, AI makes the whole image so the lighting is consistent, the person looks like they are situated in the environment. It looks natural. What you have to be careful of is when you place your product, the lighting follows the AI image in direction and in color.

Unlike most mockups, I liked this AI generated image because it is an action shot. I liked that the shirt is untucked and the jeans are ripped. The model is intensely focused on his painting, not square to the camera

smiling. I prompted that his back be to the camera because it is an allover print t-shirt.

The steps to getting the product on the image are the same I have shown previously. In addition, I have included a few examples of how the background was expanded. I will address it in more detail later. This image, which was a square AI generation originally, needed to be in a horizontal format for the layout design. Rather than crop it and lose image, I added background. Sometimes Photoshop "Content-Aware" works but most of the time I have to improvise to fill the background believably.

Above, finished image in the proportions it was designed. Right, close-up of the finished image showing the t-shirt on the figure.

STEPS

1. The original AI generation.

2. The manufacturer image of the product shot flat in studio on a white background, which was easily removed using the selection tools and deleting.

3. A black mask was created on a Photoshop layer by hand selecting and filling—no auto select tools used. I wanted a crisp edge on the mask.

4. Studying the shape of the shirt in the AI image, the product image is shaped using the Edit>Transform tools. The neckband required special attention. The sleeve seam needed to align approximately. I often use the "Warp" tool to get fabric in the right shape for a garment.

5. Using the black mask, the shape was selected then the shirt from the AI image was copied and pasted onto a new layer. This will be used to give the shirt shape and shadow.

6. The black mask was selected again and the extra image around the product was deleted leaving a shape that matches the shirt in the AI image. The AI shape layer is on top of the product layer and in the layer menu "Multiply" is selected. Opacity is adjusted until it looks right. If the AI shirt layer is not giving me enough shadow even at 100%, I sometimes copy this layer and have two shape layers active. I back down the opacity on one of them until the image looks good.

7-9 These images show how the background was extended for this image. On the right a selection was scaled to fill the background. On the left, small sections of the background were selected and filled using copying and the "Content-Aware" fill.

Here are two more examples of replacing fabric patterns in AI generated photos. The yellow dress image was placed over the AI, fitted to it. The original white dress was masked, copied and used for shape and shadow in exactly the same way as the previous pictures. One difference here, I did not like folds of the fabric so I generated another AI image just for the hip and put it into this picture.

The model in the purple dress was generated wearing a white halter top dress. This allows the straps of the replacement product dress to be positioned freely without worrying about retouching original garment straps that might be in the way. The same steps were then followed as for the t-shirt to place a product image of the dress on her.

Extending an image: Sideboard

Many of my pictures required extending because the original AI was a square and I needed a horizontal rectangle for the layout design. When the image is straight on, like the grey room on this page, it is easier to extend than when the room is at an angle. You can copy a bit of baseboard, for instance, then scale it horizontally quite easily. A flat color wall scales easily.

Plank floors are a little harder, but not impossible. If you have a section of clean floor to work with in your image, then you can copy it and manipulate it to fill in the extending floor. You have to be mindful of perspective, making sure the way the boards are placed, sized make sense. If there is no good floor to work with in the picture, I go out and generate empty AI rooms with the type of floor I need. Sometimes it is easier to just replace the whole floor rather than patch bits of it to create the extended image.

The image above is the finished image with the products in place. At the top right, the image shows the pieces that were created to make the extension left and right. The original AI generated room that I started with is on the bottom right.

Extending an image: Living Room

This is another image that required a horizontal orientation for the layout. In extending the room on the left side I had to go out and generate an AI image of a table rather than try to build off the small piece of a table in the image. On the right hand side it was easy to copy a section of the couch and then scale it horizontally.

In the end, I took an afghan from another AI image rather than use the one here. I found this one didn't shape well so I replaced it. I found enough floor to work with in this image so was able to match it in the left side of the image extension.

Because I had created masks for all of the product replacements, it was no problem to change the fabric design at the end and use a different fabric pattern. Another advantage of using masks in this process.

The image above is the finished room image. Top left, is an image of the pieces that I created to extend the room left and right and to place the products. At the bottom right is the original image I started with.

Extending an image: Bedroom

I liked this original AI image, though the lamp was generated strangely. I was able to get that back together. Other than that, this was actually a pretty straightforward job. I grabbed a piece of the curtains from the original AI, scaled it, lightened it and then used it to make the extension of the image. I used part of the floor image to create the extension, skewing the boards' direction to follow perspective.

I was able to easily extend the left side of the image by copying a section of the bed, rug and wall and scaling it. Since it was straight to the camera, it was easy to extend.

The original bed and pillows were not white so I could not isolate and use those elements to create shape and shadow. I had to freehand it. I masked the comforter to use it for the shape to place my product comforter. For both the pillows and comforter, I created shadows using the AI original image as a guide.

The image above is the finished room. Top left, is an image of the pieces that I created to extend the room left and right and to place the products. At the bottom right is the original AI generated image that I started with.

Extending an image:
Living Room

This blue room is another image that was extended. The chair was removed and the floor, wall and shadow extended in addition to putting the products in the image.

The wall was easy to extend. I copied and pasted a section in place, then scaled it horizontally. To align the shadows of the extension to the original wall, I skewed the extension vertically until they aligned.